MW00966057

Out Behind the Barn on Cicero Farm

Out Behind the Barn on Cicero Farm

Thomas A. Cicero, Jr.

FirstPublish
A Division of the Brekal Group, Inc.
control your own destiny

Copyright © 2001 by Thomas A. Cicero, Jr.
All rights reserved. Printed in the United States of America.
No part of this publication may be reproduced, stored in
a retrieval system, or transmitted, in any form or by any
means, electronic, mechanical, photocopying, recording,
or otherwise, without the prior written permission of the author.

ISBN
1-931743-01-0

Thomas A. Cicero, Jr.
Out Behind the Barn on Cicero Farm

10 9 8 7 6 5 4 3 2 1

FIRSTPUBLISH
A Division of Brekel Group, Inc.
300 Sunport Ln.
Orlando, FL 32809
407-240-1414
www.firstpublish.com

Where do you really start when you write a compilation of American Farm real life experiences? I guess being the author it has to be my decision, so be it. Like any recipe you need basic ingredients, those are first the family, the love of the land, and hard work, of course many more ingredients can be added but this is what is basic about the American Farmer. The word recipe makes you think of homemade cookies and other favorite foods, well essentially that's what this story is all about, a history lesson on a very important part of life food production.

Here it is the year 2001, well there has been a lot of change in the last 50 years, but we all still need to buy groceries. The farmer still has to work the land and tend to his animals. So this being the case I think you might enjoy my little story of how it was to grow up on a small family farm in rural America. Maybe after reading my little story you might just have a different perspective on farmers, families, and society. Hopefully you will recognize how we are all important ingredients of a very important recipe called life.

Well let me get started, back in the 1950's things were just a little simpler. Of course you do not need me to tell you that. The nice thing about them "Old Days" was that without modernization on the farm more hand work took place and Mother, Father, Sister, Brother all had a hand in getting the chores done. This I think made families communicate with each other. During the course of chores everyone worked as a team, now and then there was the occasional squabble, of course always some learning and believe it or not even some fun. The farm family worked together for another important reason, "economic survival." I think this fact played a role in children learning at an early age the importance of helping. Something else happened while all this was going on, a strong sense of love not only develops within the family but for their farm as well. Farm animals take on names, fields become portraits, tractors seem like old friends, and you knew your neighbor.

# Winter

It is wintertime. The fields are covered with a pure white blanket of snow, as you look out of the window of the warm comfort of your big old farmhouse that was built during the civil war, drafty but still a lot warmer than it is outside. But you know the calves have to be fed along with the cows; Dad has already left for the barn to throw the corn silage down the chute from the silo for feeding time. You get your heavy work clothes on and boots, then holler to Ma that your going to the barn, she yells back "careful" with a smile, she is starting supper. As you go out the cold crisp air bites your face and you hear the crunch of the frozen snow beneath your feet with every step.

Once in the barnyard you smell the sweet smell of the corn silage in the air. Dad is up in the silo forking each forkful down the chute, and you can see the steam rise into the air as he digs it out of the silo, each time a fork full is dropped down you can hear the chopped cob of the corn hit the galvanized metal chute with a roar of its own. Once in the barn you hear the cows all balling and looking to be fed after all the sweet smell is driving them crazy. So you get your wheelbarrow and fork in the silo room where the pile of fresh thrown down silage is getting higher and you start loading it up to roll it out the mangers in front of the stanchions, as you get to each cow they stick there nose in the wheelbarrow and try to tip the whole load over, one wheelbarrow will feed three cows. The smell

3

was so sweet along with the warmth it gave off actually made you wonder what it would taste like, perhaps pretty good! The cows sure did love it, especially when a measure of grain was put on top of it, sort of like an ice cream Sunday with a cherry on top. This feed of course provided the nutrients for the cows to milk to the best of their ability.

While the cows ate, Dad would get the hay in place to feed them after milking, and I would set the milking machines in the milk house and get all other milking equipment ready. Then Dad and I would sit on a bale of hay or lean on a stanchion stall petition and chat about whatever, when the cows were done eating we would start milking each of them, we ran three machines, even though the machine did the actual milking we had to start each tit by hand and wash the udder as well, four tits per cow times 50 cows meant we had to pull two hundred tits! Sometimes the cows did not like to be milked and would try to kick us. Dad had a trick for this though he would hold the tail of the cow straight up while I put the machine on her this prevented her from raising her leg to kick. This was just one of many tricks Dad knew when a job had to get done. The smell of the sweet fresh pearl white milk when you poured it out of the machine into the pail to be carried to the bulk was especially attractive to the barn cats so we would have to give them some, of course. The steady howling of the milk pump went on along with the sound of the clicking rhythm of the milking machine, until each and every cow was milked.

Once done, I would wash the equipment while Dad started feeding the hay to the cows. Then we would head up to the house with our dog Spot close behind, our boots crunching the snow as we walked, looking towards the light of the house knowing Ma was getting supper ready to put on the table. As soon as we opened the door to go in we could smell the aroma of supper. We freshened up and changed our clothes, Ma didn't have to call us a second time when it was time to eat!

The evening would be spent reading, watching TV, playing music or maybe teasing our dog Spot. Ma would knit or sew while watching TV and talking to Dad. When us kids were all home we would all sit around for awhile in the front room watching TV or sometimes play a board game, have a snack and go to bed. Simple and perhaps boring to some, but to us we knew what we could count on, which was that we were a family.

Morning would come fast. If old enough we would go down and help with chores before school. If too young we would get ready for school and visit with Ma, sometimes we would check our homework until the school bus come rolling down the road. You see, farm families are just like any other family. What sort of makes us a little different is that the farm acts as the glue to keep us just a little closer. We become so close that we become part of the farm, or does the farm become part of us?

Well, you have probably realized by now that I was the one that became cemented to the farm. Dad and I just seemed to understand what it all meant, so let's get back to morning chores. Pretty much the same as afternoon chores except the barn would have to cleaned daily. After the cows were milked and fed their morning hay we would go up for breakfast, then after breakfast we would go back to the barn to clean the gutters. Being winter this was a daily job because the cows stay in the barn most the time. Sometimes the frigid cold of winter would try to stop this needed chore by freezing the motorized chain and paddles that would run along the bottom of the gutter. Once this happened it was not practical to use it, so this meant we would back the manure spreader into the barn and fork and shovel the manure into it by hand. When the harsh frigid cold would was severe enough to freeze the chain apron on the manure spreader we were reduced to the use of the wheelbarrow, where we could fit about two to three cows manure into it before we would wheel it out into the front barnyard by hand and dump it in a pile that would await until spring before it would be reloaded and spread in the field.

Winter created many other hardships on the farm. Sometimes the biting cold frigid wind would blow thru every nook and cranny of the barn. When this happened, we were not surprised to find frozen water pipes in the morning. Walking into the barn on such a morning you might even find a flooded barn, imagine the gutter filled with water as well as the feed manger in front of the cows. What would happen is that the pipes would freeze and the ice would expand them until they split. The sound of the running water flooding the barn on a frigid cold morning was not a pleasant one. The whole day would be now devoted to shoveling with the scoop shovel the water into the wheelbarrow and dumping it outside, along with cleaning the flooded manure filled gutters. We would use extra straw to bed the cows down with; the cows would drink their water right out of the manger that day as well. We would call Briggs welding, they would melt the frozen pipes and drinking cups, and we would replace broken pipes to get all back in order. One year the water line under the ground froze. Because it was plastic it could not be thawed, we had to bring a garden hose 350 feet from the house, wrap it with heat tape and insulation.

The day we had to this little job the winter wind blew 40 to 50 miles an hour and the wind chill was 50 below zero at times. We had to get water to the cows for they could drink. The rest of that winter consisted of that hose providing water to the barn. We had to water each cow by hand with a five-gallon pail that we filled with the hose that we ran into the milk house. To insure that the hose would not freeze we would leave the water running just outside the milk house; we had a glacier several feet high that formed because the weather was constantly below zero for so long, and the running water would instantly freeze where it landed. Now that I write this I do not know how we did all of these things, but believe me, your cows become part of your family because your family depends on the cows.

What made it all worth it was that pleasant surprise of a new born calf greeting you when you opened the barn door first thing in the morning. Sometimes the mother cow would freshen earlier than expected, and you would find this black and white little calf wobbly on it's feet running from cow to cow sometimes falling even in the gutter but getting up quick enough to find one of it's mother's teats to suckle on for that much needed colostrum milk that only the mother could provide. You would always hope it was a heifer calf because you could raise it and look forward to it taking it's place in the milking herd.

Sometimes calving for the mother cow was difficult and we would have to help her deliver. We had a special rope with a slip-knot that would go onto the front feet of the calf as it was coming out, we would attach it and carefully pull in order to assist the mother. There was a special feeling of urgency of helping the out with the delivery. Even the other cows would sense the excitement of what was going on. If all was normal, once the calf was born we would hold it up from behind it's front shoulders and clean it's nose and mouth out. The mother cow would look back and immediately start talking to its baby, mooing with much concern for her baby. She would then start licking the little one and cleaning it. Within a short time the calf would start to get up on it's shaky legs and start nursing and talking back to mama with a Maaa, Maaa, and we knew all was well.

Soon this new bright black and white heifer calf would have to be taught to drink from a nursing pail, and would have it own pen. We would then have to give it a name all its own. Often the name included part of the mother's name, because, yes even here, the cows and calves were all family. I guess because we took care of them we became their family but because the cows produced the milk that we sold they took care of us as well, which is the way it was supposed to be.

During the winter months the routine was often pretty much the same. Now and then you could find some extra time to start planning for spring, the thought of the days getting longer, and warmer seemed pretty nice.

Looking at the many seed catalogues that arrive in the mail also inspired the new upcoming growing season. In the winter, the pictures of the green varieties of plants looked so much greener. Then the farming magazines would have the pictures of the newest farm equipment, priced so high you could only wonder what it would be like to own it. The farm classified ads would always be read, the chick hatchery ad is one that you always get that excitement about ordering a few chicks. I remember one year as a kid I was so anxious that I did what the ad said and ordered early for spring shipment. Well guess what, we got a call in the middle of winter from the post office saying to come and pick-up the box of chirping little chicks. What a surprise! We had no choice but to go and get the little chicks.

They had to be kept warm, so we had to put them down in the basement of our house with the heat lamp over them. What a sight they were in the middle of winter, little yellow fuzzy balls with beaks on them, eating and drinking non stop, with continuous beeping. They would huddle from time to under the heat lamps and nap for a while, then stretch their little wings and open their beaks with a long yawn. These were supposed to be a springtime project with hopes of having not only our own milk but with chickens our own eggs as well. After about eight weeks we brought them down into a spare shed and set them up in their own chicken coop. The best thing we all remember is that when they matured enough to start laying eggs we had a little problem. The prettiest of the flock turned out to be the rooster; he had bright red feathers with black trim and a big red comb on top of his head and razor sharp claws on his feet, and when anybody went to get the eggs out of the nest he would charge them and dig his spurs into them and peck with his beak. So what do you do, well I sent my little sister in to get the eggs once, she still remembers it. I don't have to tell you I never got her to get the eggs again. We ended up letting the rooster have his own area away from the hens.

One amazing thing did happened though. One of the hens did sit on her nest of eggs long enough for the eggs to hatch, and we had little chicks running all around the chicken coop. Actually these chicks grew quite well. Interesting how Mother Nature takes care of the young with the help of mother hen.

 # Springtime

See what getting too anxious for spring gets you, more than just an early arrival of a baby chick order, yes it turned out to be a lot of work, but it was an adventure! Winter did finally start to come to an end and seed orders were placed and calf pens were cleaned along with fence repair supplies bought. I hope my recollection of the chicken story didn't make you lose direction of where we were with the story. It is springtime on the farm and what an exciting time! It should go without saying how busy it can get on the farm in this season of new beginnings. The household becomes busy with spring-cleaning. Ma would always look forward to this time of year, putting everyone to work washing woodwork and walls. Then a new coat of paint where needed would be brushed on by us all lending a hand. Mrs. Trescott, the wallpaper lady, would be called to set up a date for a room to be wallpapered. During the winter the new Robinson's wallpaper book had arrived. Ma, with much contemplation had the color, pattern she liked picked out, and now she would order it. While all this was going on St. Patrick's Day, corn beef and cabbage along with Irish music would help set the spirit of spring in the air. Then because of our Italian heritage on March 19, St. Joseph's Day would be celebrated. The smell of bowknot and spingee Italian cookies being baked along with fish and stuffed artichokes and aromas from all the favorite recipes filled the house.

By the time March 21 came, the first day of spring, we had already been celebrating for some time! March, being like an old lady, could not make up her mind and some old saying about her borrowing some days from February would prove true, and as the Ides of March would come and go we would have to wait for her winds to blow in the spring like weather. I suppose that is why we kept busy in the house this time of year, because until the weather really became warm enough the getting out in the fields had to wait.

The new fence post we bought in March had been stacked in a pile in the corner of the barnyard. In early April we could get the tractor and wagon, and load some up along with our trusty posthole bar and mallet, some staples and wire. Spot, our dog, would join us and we would head out into the greening pasture, to fix fence. The smell of the old pasture coming back to life was very distinct, sweet and earthy, the new tender grass shoots mixed with darker looking dandelion leaves and bright yellow blossoms looked like a succulent fresh salad, all awaiting for the first day the cows would be let back out into the pasture. This moment would depend on us getting the fence fixed and ready. So there we were the warm sunshine feeling so good on us as Dad drove the tractor and I rode the wagon down the cow lane into the pasture and along the fence line. Even Spot enjoyed the wagon ride looking for a young woodchuck or two as he rode along. Dad and I would look for poor sections of the fence as we went along, the old locust fence post mixed with more recent cedar post along with the rusty brown wire told the story of how many seasons have come and gone for this fence line. The tractor came to a halt, and off jumped Spot. He loved to explore every hole and crevice he could find while we would mend the fence.

For repairs that required a new post, first I would get the bar and proceed to make a hole. Then Dad would get the post and set it in and with the use of the mallet we would pound it in. After I thought we were done Dad would always grab the top of it and wiggle it, and of course as always a couple more hits were needed. Only after Dad would spit in his hands, would he grab the handle of the mallet and give it those last couple wallops. Sometimes he hit so hard that the top of the post would split a little. It was solidly planted now and we could proceed to staple the wire to it. As we went along the sound of post being pounded in would echo through the valley. As we worked Dad would be reminiscence of the old days, recalling the names of some of the cows that always would get out of the pasture, some how they would find a hole in the fence and lead the herd out for an exciting time, perhaps the saying "the grass always looks greener on the other side of the fence," got it's start from the cows getting out!

The many springtime chores included loading the stockpiles of manure with the Farmall H tractor and loader into the manure spreader and spreading this valuable organic fertilizer, sweet smell and all, out into the fields that were to be soon plowed. There was a special, exciting feeling about everything that we did, renewed not only a new growing season but also a tradition that was part of our lives. To describe the true essence of a family working along with nature would be a difficult task to do. There are so many intricate facets of this miraculous endeavor that seem to grow just as a seed that the farmer plants. Along with all of the work came the many little rewards that nature provides, after all as a farmer, working close to nature you get to see it up close and first hand.

All of this springtime activity kept us very busy, along with barn chores and milking time, gave us a well rounded out day on the farm. Then there were the additional activities such as knowing when a cow had to be bred and calling Bruce Van Loon, the technician. Then the occasional need for Ken Kiehle DVM to check on a cow or calf. Keeping track of the weekly mobile grain grinding truck and making sure the grain was mixed the way you wanted. Dansville Farm Supply owned by Moses Garippa provided this service, Fred was the driver and Don handled the bags. Then as years went by we had GLF, a farmer owned co-op provide this service. Eventually their name changed to Agway.

Whenever we had a cow to sell or a calf to go to market it was Dick Farrell we would call. He would always pull in with his big IH truck to load them up, which with some cows took a trick or two. We had a visit every day from the milkman, Pete Gilbert, who hauled milk for our farmer owned Conesus Milk Co-op. Another milk hauler by the name of Charlie Minnehan that hauled for another milk co-op would always seem to drive by the road at the same time with a friendly wave and smile. It was a good feeling seeing our milk on its way to becoming cheese, milk and ice cream. One thing that I can tell you with certainty, is that all these people that would come to our farm sort of became old friends in time. I think the fact that we were all interdependent on each other along with that old fashion belief that seemed to prevail with farmers that hard work and trust went hand in hand. Visiting and friendly talk always would take place and in fact it was expected. Time was always made for socializing just enough to even find out what was new with a neighbor. Springtime added even more time to visit when we had a chance. After all, the weather was warmer and standing around talking just a little seemed to go along with it. The life of the farmer seems to have it's own little world.

Every day has a new adventure down on the farm, such as making repairs to various farm equipment and getting them ready for spring fieldwork. Father and son making a trip to Day Implement to get tractor parts, and then going to Webb Implement for plow parts. If for some reason neither of these places had the part we needed, we took a trip to "Uncle" Bill Knapp's, because he would have it. Each place had a special smell, perhaps oil and grease from the mechanics shop or the many new pieces of fresh painted parts from the factory, but one thing for sure was that it became an expected odor to look forward to when there. Upon entering the store you could always expect a friendly hello from Sy Day. Dad would give me a dime for a Coke from the machine, and that Coke was always the coldest and the best. New farm equipment literature was free for the taking, so while we would wait for a part number or the customer in line in front of us we enjoyed the colorful pictured brochures. If there happened to be a good looking piece of used equipment on the floor or in the yard we would give it a going over, and if it interested us enough we would ask the price. Most often that would be the end of our curiosity.

I'll never forget over at the John Deere Dealer, Stub Webb urged my Dad and I to look at a used 3020 tractor. He told me to get up on it; he didn't have to ask twice. Stub started it and showed me the features. The bright yellow cushioned seat, the rich green fenders, the bold style of the newer designed grill, and the powerful roar of the diesel engine. When Dad and I went home that afternoon we didn't talk too much, we both knew that tractor would help us get field work done, no doubt about it. The next day after much worry about spending the money we decided to trade the John Deere 60 in for the 3020. The excitement of this bold decision is something to be remembered, because it marked the real beginning of me starting to take over the majority of the fieldwork.

Since Dad sort of liked to use the smaller tractor, an IH 424, I got to take over the use of this big green farming machine. The IH 424 was a tractor Dad bought new from Sy Day the IH dealer and this tractor was a tough little red power house and very useful for many farm chores. Dad had a special look of pride when he was on it; I can still picture him just humming along on it. Springtime this year took a big step in the direction of transition, new generation in a small way starting to take the reigns, thus not only renewing a new season but a new farming generation.

Plowing Time

With the soil conditions in the fields, we knew by instinct it was time to start plowing. A sense of accomplishment for having the manure spread and fences fixed along with other things that need to be done, made us happy that we were ready. Well the moment that I had been waiting for had finally arrived and with Dad's go ahead look, I jumped up on our John Deere 3020, turned the key, pushed the starter and listened to the two powerful 12 volt batteries turn that 75 hp diesel engine over. As the diesel engine turned, black smoke would flow out of the flapping cap of the exhaust pipe. This powerful motor, ever so slowly came to life with every revolution of the starter. Sitting on that bright yellow seat, looking at the gauges I could feel the power of this big green tractor when the engine ignited with a powerful roar. Dad looked on with the excitement of a kid, there was an unspoken sense of pride when this 3020 came to life. A father proud of his son, commanding the controls of this big tractor, and I looked at Dad, knowing what this moment meant to the both of us. The three-bottom plow was already hooked up, so I raised it up with the control lever. Dad gave last minute instruction of what field to start plowing and what spots to look out for in that particular field that might cause a problem such as getting stuck. I then put the tractor in gear, opened the throttle, and with a roar and a puff of diesel smoke began my drive down the gravel driveway to the field that nestled itself in this pretty valley farm.

Along the way, one could not help to admire the beauty that this season puts forth. The bright green grass, glistening with the dew that still remained where it was shaded by the trees with their swelling buds and fresh opened delicate dainty leaves. The robins at work making their nests would take flight as the roar of the tractor approached each shrub and tree that I passed by. The warmth of the early morning sun felt so good on my back, but also fueled with much excitement the promise of good weather to help me and my tractor get this field plowed. Then all of a sudden a red fox jumped out of the brush as I drove across the sluice that allowed the crystal clear sparkling water to flow in the creek as I drove over the top of it. I would always have to slow the speed down on the tractor when going over this part of the driveway where the creek passed thru, otherwise the tractor and I would bounce like a basketball. Once over, I would open up the throttle to keep up a good steady pace to the field I was headed for. Spot was running way up ahead of the tractor. Upon approaching the field I noticed that Spot had his job already cut out, once again he caught a woodchuck out of his hole and was keeping him at bay, barking and running circles around the woodchuck. Spot would tire out the furry groundhog this way; sometimes he would bark almost all day before he would be able to make his move.

Once in the field I would give it a good looking over. Some weeds were already growing with the corn stalks left from last year's crop. I drove across the field to check for wet areas and to make sure ground conditions were just right. Then I would look to the other end of the field and find that certain tree, like the sights of a rifle, I would take aim. Then being in the center of the field I would look to my right and then to my left. If the distance looked about equal on each side then I would lower my plow. Once my plow was in the ground and you could feel the pull of the soil being turned over. I would keep my eye on that tree at the other end and hope I was plowing straight down the center. With a quick jerk of the throttle my big green tractor would lunge forward spewing a big cloud of diesel fuel exhaust along with a roar that made the hairs on the back of your neck stand up and you dared not look anywhere but upon that distant tree you picked as your sights. This first trip down the field always seemed the most exciting. Once you reached the other end, you could not seem to turn around quick enough to head back. This first strike of the land was just the beginning of going back and forth countless times, raising and lowering the plows each time; it all became mechanical.

Nature and all it had to offer was everywhere you looked. Fresh plowed soil, rich with earthy aroma, revealed the various forms of life that it sustained. The many bright pink earthworms wiggling, then the many different kind of insects that were crawling frantically in all different directions, quite disturbed at being exposed. Their world was literally now turned upside down now that the soil was turned over by the plow. Within a short time the many different variety of birds would soon keep me company in the field feasting on this delicious menu that seemed to be quite pleasing to their taste.

There were the robins with their bright orange breast, the red wing black bird, the large black crows, and the bright colorful orange and black Baltimore oriole. Bird after bird would take their turn carefully scouting the fresh turned soil, the sound of the roaring tractor seemed to draw them rather than scare them away. As I observed all this winged activity, I noted the lone seagull hovering high above in the clear blue sky, circling, as any good scout would do. Without doubt the miracle of Mother Nature some how provides very keen instinctive sense to this species. Whenever enough land has been freshly turned over it almost seems without fail a scout is attracted to the field. Within a short while, one by one they start to appear in the bright blue sky until there are so many they become like an army. They squawk so loud their sound is heard above the noise of the tractor. They follow very close behind the plow; flying very low, ready to swoop down quickly to snatch up a morsel of what the earth had to offer for their meal. Now the field was covered with bright white sea gulls, hundreds behind me and the tractor, and hundreds flying around the tractor, just above my hat and even trying to land on the fenders. So many appear so quickly this invasion without question puts a little bit of reservation on my behalf of whether these white gliders might mistaken me for a meal. When they have satisfied their initial hunger they settle down a bit, then I can really start to enjoy the company of this dependable guest whose presence seem to crown all the glory of that first day of plowing.

Of course barn chores still exist and the cows have to be milked. With the weather being good though Dad would hold the fort down in the barn. I would come up from the field for milking and after supper go back out sometimes until dusk. If field conditions were just right this was the time to get that jump on an early crop that could only be planted if the plowing and fitting were done.

Spring plowing was sometime filled with much unwanted adventure. Each field that was plowed had characteristics all of its own, from that hidden boulder that lay beneath the soil but still high enough to catch your plow point and stop your tractor right in your tracks, to that wet spot where you would sink in and there you would stay. Now these wet spots not only created fear of getting stuck but also created a challenge that made you and your tractor become a team. Your tractor's capability of pulling the plow in a higher gear increased your speed enough to create enough momentum to keep moving through the sticky wet spot, along with your skill as operator to regulate the depth of the plow, is what kept you plowing. Sometimes you had to use good judgment and not plow through the wet spot but go around it. When your decision proved wrong you would find yourself up to the tractor's axle in mud, and the more you spun your tires the deeper you went in. Walking back to the barn to tell Dad you hit quick sand was not my idea of fun. Dad would give a chuckle and start gathering up rope and chains along with a clevis to hook up for the tow with another tractor. Now Dad and I were the team working together to pull our tractor and plow out of that muddy wet spot that this time had won the challenge. With a tug of the chain the power of both tractors surged forward, Dad looking back at me steering my big green plowing machine as he would open the throttle up on his smaller red IH 424 as that little tractor pulled with all its might. With wheels spinning and engines roaring, father and son working as one united by the chain that connected the two tractors, feeling the thrill of success as the big green plowing machine climbed out of the deep ruts and onto solid ground. Words between Dad and I did not have to be spoken: we both felt a great sense of accomplishment. I don't need to tell you that these experiences taught me great respect for wet areas in the field. In other words stay away from them if you could!

Spring kept us busy but never too busy to enjoy all it had to offer. Sitting out on the porch after a delicious supper, talking family talk and listening to the peepers sing. They sounded like a chorus as their melodious song echoed thru the valley and seemed to get louder as the sun set and darkness fell upon the countryside.

Day to day activities this time of year took second place to field-work. Planting of the crops was the goal in order to insure another years supply of feed and income. The excitement of hooking on to the grain drill to plant oats, along with Charlie from Agway making the fertilizer delivery first thing in the morning, excitement filled the air with a sense of what was to be accomplished this sunny bright glorious day.

Dad hooked up to the wagon with the load of fertilizer and oat seed. I put my 3020 in gear and we were off to the field where we would spend the day going round and round, and up and down the field until it was all planted. Around noon Ma would bring us lunch, as we all sat down under the shade of the hickory tree on the green spring grass and had our little picnic I knew this was a special time to enjoy.

With the roar of the tractor, the singing of the discs on the drill as they turned dropping their seed and a cloud of dust following behind, the field was planted. We would go up, wash and have a snack before milking. After supper Dad would hook up to the cultipacker to roll the seedbed. Dad always seemed to enjoy rolling the field to a smooth level look and thus he put the finishing touch on the days work.

Now that the oats were planted the race was on to get the corn seed in and sprouting! If the weather cooperated, that is exactly what we did. Row after row you could hear the clicking of the IH corn planter dropping the seed into the rich fertile soil, field after field. Dad was planting today so I had the fun of opening fertilizer bags and sitting on the wagon. Bright blue was the sky, so I laid back on the wagon and looked up at it. It seemed the longer I would stare into the aqua blue atmosphere the farther I could see up, until a big white billowing cloud that looked like a sail on a boat went by. If you stayed still and kept looking straight up it felt as if you were moving rather than the clouds. The glowing warmth of the sun bathing you from all directions along with the gentle wisp of a breeze gave me an experience that only Mother Nature can provide. Here I was working but yet enjoying what vacationers pay to enjoy! With the completion of planting came the meticulous job of cleaning up of the equipment and storing it away. Now it was up to Mother Nature to do her job by providing the warm gentle soaking rains along with the sun's brilliant rays that would provide much needed warmth for young seedlings to grow. We as farmers had done our part now it would be " The Lord Willing" as Dad would always say.

With summer now near, along came Mom and Dad's anniversary, Flag Day, birthdays, first day of summer and graduation time. Sometimes we would have a cousin's graduation party to attend. With the spring work done it was a nice change of pace to be able to socialize and tell a little story about some of our many adventures we experienced this last spring during planting time.

Now of course being a dairy farmer meant you had cows. Whenever they decided to stretch the fence more than it could go, these cows would go out on a picnic all of their own. More than once we got a call from a neighbor that our cows were out. One time I remember being at a summer wedding and just before it was time to sit down for the dinner a hostess came in and announced that our cows were out. I guess it was a good thing a good neighbor knew how to track us down. As long as we are talking about the cows getting out I will share one more story about the time we heard mooing right outside our house windows just before sunrise. Now if that doesn't get you out of bed in a hurry!

Imagine a large black and white head with ears to match staring back at you as you peered with surprise out your bedroom window! Not to mention the fact that Creamela had a big mouthful of our once pretty flowers that were planted ever so neatly around the foundation of the house. She looked very content just chomping away without a care, actually seemed to have a smile as she looked through the window back at us.

We definitely were not very happy about the prospect of chasing the cows around the yard with the road being so near. This is when the whole family works frantically together jumping and hollering and keeping our arms and hands extended in order to herd the cows together and direct them down the barn. Once we get them locked in their stanchions in the barn, with much anxiety we count them to make sure they are all there. This time we were delighted to find they were, because there have been times we had to go out looking for the rampaging mavericks.

Haying Time

The month of June for us is traditionally the time of year we start haying. The clover, alfalfa and other grasses have reached maturity but still have the color green. To the dairy farmer the color green means protein value for the milk cow. Good quality hay can make a big difference in milk production and that means a direct effect on our pocket book. If a farmer wants to stay in business he has to conduct himself like a businessman by farming in an efficient and productive manner. So with emphasis on quality feed and good production I think it is easy to understand now why a family works so hard to get the hay crop up and in the barn.

With school out for the summer that meant some schoolboys would be looking to earn a few extra dollars. We would have some boys start out working for us stacking hay as early as Junior High and come back every summer all through High School. It was a growing experience in many ways. When they first came their voices would be high pitched, then the changing stage to that deep and grown up. Stacking hay weeded out the slackers. The boys who became dependable became more than help as we all worked putting up the hay through the years. Hard work, sweat and hay shaft along with that cold drink under the shade of a tree in the hayfield seemed to be important ingredients for long lasting fond memories and unspoken bonds of friendship. Just last year a former hay stacker stopped by. It was some twenty odd years since he last held

21

a bale of hay. But here he was, stopped by our sweet corn stand out front of the house, then came to the door with his children to say hi. Then from out of nowhere he asked if he could walk around the old farm with the kids and tell them of his haying days on the Cicero Farm. Why of course was my answer, an old friend had came back. I introduced him to my son who in turn was the recipient of many old haying stories as he accompanied him and walked around the barnyard listening to him recalling his fond memories.

There are many such hay stackers throughout the community that this farm has given them more than their wages. Their wages are now long gone but an important learning experience lives on. Putting up hay is sort of a science. A farmer listens to the weatherman, even though he is right maybe only half the time. So Dad and I would also look to the sky to find some fair weather clouds, then of course watch the sunset (red sky at night sailors delight), the direction of the wind, and check for a halo around the moon. See I told you that you had to be a scientist to be a farmer!

Well by gosh we had to start cutting hay sometime, the saying is you got to cut it to bale it. One last inspection of our New Holland Haybine completed our readiness. Jumped up on my John Deere 3020 and was off to the hayfield. Spot sensed the excitement and followed close behind smelling and checking every bush along the way. The clear blue sky promised it to be a sun filled day. A gentle summer breeze now and then assured that the hay would dry fast as it was cut.

Once in the field, the task of putting the haybine in cutting position had to be done before I could begin. Spot watched attentively, just as anxious to get the show on the road. After all he was going to hunt for woodchucks as the hay was being cut. He knew once the tall grass was out of the way these critters would not have any place to hide as they scattered about if they got caught out of their hole as the haybine made it's pass. Round and round we went as we cut the field. The grasshoppers jumped along my path with a steady rhythm, sometimes landing right on me! The smell of fresh cut hay soon filled the air. Now and then a colorful butterfly would land on a snow white daisy and would fly off just in time, as the haybine would go by. The steady sound of the machine running seemed to sing a song as you listened to it. Listening to your machine was important, because you could tell if it was about to plug up with hay by the sound and could slow it up in time for it would not plug up. As the insects flew in all directions as the machine met the grass, gold finches, robins, sparrows would catch them in mid air. Sometimes I was visited by a group of swallows. They would fly circles around the tractor, as they would catch the tiny hoppers. These birds sometimes would get a little too close I would think, but they just kept about their business.

One time as I was cutting hay, all of a sudden a large shadow appeared over the tractor and me. I looked up and guess what I saw? For the very first time I saw an eagle, with a wingspan of eight feet, flying right above the tractor and me. At first I thought it wanted to make me supper! Then all of a sudden it swooped down and grabbed a rabbit as it ran out from the hay I was cutting. This magnificent and majestic bird picked this rabbit right up with its powerful claws and carried it a few hundred feet in the air to the hedgerow where I guess he had his supper. I was glad he was done hunting for the day!

Spot, who had been faithfully running round and round the field all day with me, caught a woodchuck out of his hole. Now Spot deserted me and started his constant barking at this brown furry creature. Spot was beagle size so he had to wear out his opponent before he made the move. Sometimes you would hear him barking down in the hayfield, running circles and putting the scare into this furry woodchuck until after the afternoon milking time. When the barking stopped we knew Spot had done his job.

With the hay cut now we had to wait a day before we would turn it over into windrows with our New Idea hay rake. The hay has to dry on the one side before you can turn it over. This is why good drying weather is so important. That evening as we sat on the front porch of the house, the aroma of new cut hay was in the air. The field was in the middle of the farm but that did not stop that sweet smell from finding it's way all the way to our front porch!

We kept busy the following morning with milking and barn chores, but found time before lunch for Dad and I to make a trip to Parnell's New Holland Dealer in Greigsville for some shear pin bolts and baler twine. It was always fun to visit the dealership because they always had new equipment to learn about. We often took home brochures about the new machinery to read and of course dream about. The tractor dealers, whether Webb Implement, Kingston Farm Equipment, or my favorite Sy Day IH Implement right here in Livonia, all had a special smell of parts, supplies and new tractors. The Coke machines at these dealers always had the little bottles that kept the pop so cold it was partially frozen, and it goes without saying it was the best. Of course we always put our coin in the coke machine whenever we went for parts for that special treat!

Sometimes the hay equipment would break right in the middle of the field. Dad and I would study it, and see if we could fix it ourselves. Sometimes we could, but if we couldn't, we would call on Leonard Briggs. He was a dependable mechanic who would come right out to the field.

After we got back from getting parts we had lunch. Ma always seemed to find something good for lunch. We would talk about our trip while we ate. When finished, Dad would then go and hook up the IH 424 tractor to the hay rake and off he was to rake the hay. I would put air in the wagon tires then bring them to the field and check on Dad and see how the drying hay looked. As I parked the wagon and disconnected it I could hear the squeaking of the hay rake as it turned the grasses over. The sound got louder and louder as Dad approached the end of the field that I was at. He had a big smile on his face; he was pleased with the hay being so dry and told me it should be ready tomorrow for baling.

Cows in the pasture in the spring.

Cows grazing in the fall.

John Deere 3020:
"The big green farming machine"

**Winter chores with the International Harvester
450 and spreader.**

A sweet corn field nearing maturity.

**Cicero family at combine time: Tom, son
Matthew, and nephew Joey.**

Dad on his 424 pulling a self-unloading wagon at silo filling time.

Spot, our faithful farm dog.

Baling Time

That morning we were up just a bit earlier to get milking and chores done. The cows were out of the barn and out to pasture in no time. Milking machines washed and up for breakfast! I was then on the phone to the high school boys that wanted to work. Sometimes if their parents could not bring them over, Dad or I would go pick them up. With the baler greased and the help having arrived it was off to the field to get started. The start of the tractor signaled the help to get on the wagon that Dad was bringing down behind the baler and me. Before you knew it, the wagon was hitched to the baler, the PTO lever that engaged the hay baler was pushed, and the big flywheel was turning. Burumm, burumm, was the steady sound of the flywheel turning the plunger in the baler pushing the hay along as it was made into a square seventy five pound bale. As I drove the tractor a steady back and forth motion with each push of the plunger set a steady rhythm for all of us to feel as the machine did it's work. Round the field we went as the baler ate up the raked windrows. The boys carefully stacked each square bale just as you would building blocks. A well stacked load assured it's arrival to the hay barn in one piece. If the bales were not stacked properly they would loosen, come apart and come off the wagon as it was towed along the path back to the barn.

Summer's hot sun shined down making it a hot afternoon. The boys were wet with sweat and the hay shaft was sticking to them.

After each load we would take a break and have a drink of some cold ice water out of the cooler. That water break seemed like an oasis in the desert! Dad was transporting each load to the barn for unloading by the other crew at the hay barn. The use of a hay conveyer eased the work at the wagon but up in the haymow it was hot for the boys stacking in the loft. That particular day we unloaded each load once and loaded it again in order to get it all up and either in the barn or left on the wagon to be unloaded another day. As dusk set in that night, and we approached the hay wagons to cover with a tarp, you could smell the captured sunshine in each and every bale on the wagon. You knew this coming winter this hay would be mighty good tasting to the cows!

Old Shelly

On a small dairy farm you raise all your heifer calves born from your best cows. In each herd there are always certain family lines that seem to carry on such good traits that these cow families sometimes have grandmother, mother, daughter all milking in the herd at the same time. We had such a cow family that came from the Rag Apple line. The Grandmother's name was Old Shelly. She would milk two pails of milk morning and night, a very productive cow indeed. So was her daughter Shelly and granddaughter Young Shelly. This cow family line produced large framed cows with big udders and longevity. These cows stayed so long in the herd they became part of our family just as an old faithful family dog would.

Old Shelly was sixteen years old and heavy with calf. We had noticed her age was slowing her up but we just could not let her go to market. We had hoped for one more lactation. One early summer morning when we let the cows in the barn for feed and milking, we noticed Old Shelly did not come in the barn. Dad went looking for her out in the pasture. He found her in the hollow, a somewhat protected area she had picked to have her baby. She had not delivered as of yet, so we coaxed her closer to the side of the barnyard. We left her alone, because sometimes mother cows do better on their own.

With the milking completed we checked on her progress. The back legs of the calf were showing so we got a rope and put a slip-knot over the unborn calf's exposed feet. Old Shelly knew we were going to help her out, as we gently pulled she pushed and together we brought another generation of the Rag Apple line into the world. A large framed heifer calf was soon bouncing around and drinking off her loving mother, as mother licked and cleaned her new baby.

The following morning when we let the cows in again Old Shelly did not come in the barn. Usually they come in with their baby sometimes following close behind, but not this time. So once again Dad went to look for her and found her on the north side of the barnyard. Her calf was sleeping next to her. Old Shelly seemed to look all right, so we tried to get her up to get her in the barn. We tried and tried but with no success. So we called Dr. Ken Kiehle, our vet. We went on to complete the morning milking, and just as we let the cows out of the barn, Dr. Kiehle pulled in the driveway. We immediately brought him to Old Shelly, and after checking her over he concluded she had a calcium deficiency or some call it "milk fever." He gave her a shot and some medicine. He told us because of her age he just did not know if he could help her replace all the calcium she lost between the calf and her milk production. But he said he would come back the next day to check and for us to feed her and take the calf in the barn and give it milk replacer. So with much hope we followed his instructions, because if anyone could help her it was Doc Kiehle.

Almost a week had gone by with Old Shelly not able to get up on all four legs. We relieved some milk pressure from her udder by rolling her from one side to the other. The vet advised us to try lifting her with a special device he brought over for us to use with a pulley and winch set up. This was to be done daily to see if it would help her gain confidence on her own to get up if she had the ability to do so. We made all this special effort because this cow was not just any old cow. But eventually the decision of letting her go had to be made. When that time came we called Dick Farrell. Our relationship with him as our livestock dealer had taught us he would know how to get Old Shelly on his truck in a humane way for she could be put to rest. He understood our feelings about this old cow, being a farmer as well, and had the experience and thoughtfulness to properly load her. Old Shelly was missed but her heifer calf was named after her and went on to uphold the Rag Apple line reputation of milk production. Once again renewal assured tradition to continue.

Summer

With it being the month of July that meant a family picnic on the fourth and watching the Conesus Lake of Fire that lit up the sky in the western horizon of our farm. Our dog Spot would go crazy with fear at the sounds of all the fireworks, the loud explosive bang along with the whistle that sometime followed each shower of brilliant colors was more than he could figure out.

Hemlock Fair time was fast approaching as well. Jack Slattery and George Haefner of the Rochester radio station WHAM were announcing it quite regular over the radio we had in the barn that we listened to during milking time. It was believed that having a radio in the barn relaxed the cows, which in turn caused them to have better milk let down. We enjoyed the radio whether the cows did or not!

I can remember my brothers Joe and John getting their heifer calves Thorndale and Creamela ready for the fair. They had to be washed, brushed, and rubbed with Linseed oil to make them shine, along with practice leading them with a halter. So busy with the heifers were Joe and John that forgot they needed white pants for themselves for judging time. Well a fast trip downtown to our local and reliable J.C. Monte Clothing Store remedied that little problem. They received red and yellow ribbons for all the effort, but the memory of the accomplishment is the true treasure.

Our Uncle Jimmy watched the gate with other veterans. Sometimes he let us into the fair with just a nod and a smile! New farm machinery on display, along with the Hemlock Fire Dept. sugared coated waffles were my favorite parts of the fair. Once the fair was over you knew combine time was near.

Combine Time

Wheat and oats, both small grains, needed to be harvested this time of year. The machine that did the work was called a combine. When the grain was ripe there was always a sense of urgency to harvest it before the head of golden grain would sprout. Wheat was mainly grown on a dairy farm as a cash crop, but it became worthless for flour once it sprouted. The main concern for oats was that once it reached maximum height it tends to fall down flat in the field, and is much more difficult to combine. So now that we have an understanding of why time is of the essence, the excitement of harvest will be much better understood and appreciated.

Livonia's countryside this time of year was painted the color of gold from farm to farm. Each wheat field had it's own shape and size but gold was the color. It was a sure sign that the wheat was ready for harvest.

The Wingate Bros. Farm, the Schuster Farm, the Kurtz Farm, the Brisbane Farm all within a couple of miles of ours, not to mention My Uncle Sam's, Uncle Frank's, and Uncle Joe's farm just across from us. Then Uncle Leo and Aunt Libby's farm down the south end of our road. These were all family farms, with each and every family working together.

Combine time brought neighbor farmers together for the harvest. Whose wheat would be ready first? Sometimes a neighbor farmer needed to borrow a wagon or was in need of an extra truck with a grain box. In our case we waited for a neighbor who did custom combining. Through the years there was Dudley Reed, Ted Henry, Uncle Joe, and Ron Blowers, just to name a few, who brought that most important machine to our farm to cut the wheat. I remember one year the weather had delayed harvesting and the custom combining regulars were backed up with other farmers. So Dad went to Vince Kurtz down the road and told him our wheat would sprout if not harvested soon. The very next day Vince was up with his JI Case self-propelled combine and got the wheat in. He did not want anything in return, he was just happy to have helped. Those were the days, when neighbors practiced being good neighbors.

As kids we would play in wheat as was it unloaded into the wagon or truck. You could always count on catching the grasshoppers as they jumped amongst the many grains of wheat. We would grab the wheat by the handful and feel it's smooth hard texture; we even put a grain or two in our mouths and chew on it because they sure tasted good. We would imagine what this load of wheat would look like as flour and wonder how many loaves of bread could be made from it. As the combine unloaded its bin after its rounds in the field, the wheat got deeper in the truck and we would sink in with every step we took. We were literally swimming in wheat by the time the load was filled to the top of the grain racks on the truck. The full load of wheat was also loads of fun for us kids to play in!

The fond memories of combine time exemplify that learning, working, and fun can co-exist. Because even now as an adult working beside Dad at harvest time, I still feel the excitement as the wheat is emptied bin after bin from the combine into the truck. Of course a good harvest is economically important, and there is happiness for it, but the childhood impression made of experiencing the joy that children get from just simply playing, brought a smile to me as I thought about how much fun it used to be. The only difference now is that when I get in the wagon, it is to shovel the wheat as it unloads. Of course there still is a hint of fun as the grasshoppers remind me of my childhood.

Hemlock Agway was the destination for the unloading and sale of the wheat. The store manager would always do a moisture test of the wheat from each load, along with checking to make sure it was cleaned properly enough before it was allowed to be unloaded.

We would always pay our spring fertilizer and seed bills from the sale of the wheat. This was a very important accomplishment to help stay ahead financially. The straw from the wheat was ours to keep for use as bedding for our cows. That was now the next goal to accomplish, the baling of the straw!

Windrow after windrow wound their way round and round the field, golden colored straw piled high just waiting for me and my big John Deere and New Holland baler. With the wagon hooked up and the baler engaged the noise and dust filled the air as the baling machine hungrily ate up the bright wheat straw with big gulps and spit out bale after bale to be stacked on the wagon as we went round and round that field. Each load was a picture in itself, as the beautiful yellow straw stood out as a silhouette against the red sunset in the distant horizon. The days sunshine had been captured in each bale that now would bring warmth to the cows as bedding for them to lie down in on a cold winter's night.

With the wheat straw stacked neatly in the barn the aroma of its freshness seemed everywhere, and it sure smelled good! But soon the barn would have a different odor. Conesus Milk Co-Op notified us that the whitewash man was scheduled to whitewash the inside of our dairy barn today. So we busily covered the windows, milk pump, and exhaust fan because when the man did his job he sprayed everything. This wet lime spray was done once a year in the summer to meet sanitation requirements from our New York State milk inspector. Our farmer owned milk co-op would then deduct the cost from our milk check and pay the whitewash man. There always seemed to be enough deductions, from membership dues to the trucking charges, and advertising fees.

The milk check came every two weeks, usually the tenth and twenty-fifth of every month. We always looked forward to the checks arrival. Sometimes if we were short of funds, especially if some added expense was to arise, we would go see Thelma Arnold, the Conesus Milk Co-Op 's Lakeville office manager. She always helped many farmers by advancing them funds in between checks. She always had a friendly smile, and would chat about the weather or family.

Enough said about the milk check. Let's get back to what started this subject of money. Bad enough we had to pay for it, but we had to cleanup after the whitewash man was done as well. For days our clothes were all whitewash from just doing our regular chores in the barn. The lime would dry and rub off on everything it touched. Ma would step up her laundry chores to keep up with the messy snow-white powdery lime mess. Even the cows had additional white spots on them! But it would not be summer without this everything white time of year.

# Second Cutting

Mid-summer meant the hay fields were ready to be cut and baled again. Second cutting alfalfa was a dark rich green color and was rich in protein. This made it a highly prized feed because it helped with the cows' milk production.

The cutting and baling did not take as long as first cutting because the hay was of course much sparser in the field. But the sweet smell of the alfalfa more than made up for lack of abundance, this was the cream of the crop! Dad would say this kind of hay was like ice cream to the cows. All you had to do was watch the cows eat it and you would agree they sure did slurp it up like an ice cream cone!

The summer weather provided ideal weather for the hay to dry fast, but also provided ideal weather for family reunions and picnics. What I liked were the summer evenings when the work was done sitting out on the porch watching the lightening bugs fly all around while our family would just talk about just anything. It was a peaceful time, very relaxing. It instilled a sense of harmony within you, family and nature. Sometimes Dad would tell Ma "Let's go uptown to Long's IGA and get a package of ice cream on a stick." Well, he did not have to say it twice. Joe, John, my sister Kathy and I were in the car in an instant. The fun of going for a ride was almost just as much as a treat as the ice cream!

After second cutting usually the oats were ready for combining. Through the many years we had several farmers custom combine our oats. I remember one year a neighbor farmer by the name of Charlie Rolfe came. He had special fingers on his combine for picking up the fallen down oats in the field. He accomplished getting all our oats when he went through our field. Getting all the oats was very important but I think the neatest thing was that his daughter Pam was a classmate of mine in school.

The connection with a classmate's parent right here on our farm right in the middle of summer vacation seemed to connect the friendship I had with Pam in school, and the friendship Dad had with her father. Neighbors, friends and community, that seemed what this old farm seemed to bring together time and time again.

With grasshoppers jumping just about everywhere in the wagon and truck, both filled to the brim with oats, we jumped in and got a ride up to the wooden grain bin inside the hay barn. In the old days my brother Joe and John, along with my father, would use a galvanized bushel to scoop up the oats and dump them into the grain bin while I would help by using a broom to help gather any stray oats in the wagon. When Dad bought an electric auger the work became much easier, but still just as dusty. When the bin was full we were assured there would be a new supply of oats for grain grinding for the up coming year.

Baling of the dark golden oat straw was the excitement of the following day. This straw was much softer and more absorbent than the wheat straw. I also liked it because it was less prickly to handle when stacking. With all the cows and calves, good straw was a much-needed byproduct of the wheat and oat harvest.

This time of year, the many different kinds of bushes and wild flowers were reaching maturity. On the bushes the flowers had turned to little berries. Some bushes had orange color berries and some had red colored. These were not good for eating, but the red and black raspberries were ready to pick, and pick we did! When we had our baskets full we brought them to Ma and she made the most delicious tasting pies from this fresh wild raspberry fruit, we would top our piece of pie with vanilla ice cream and I'll leave the rest to your imagination! Queen Anne's Lace was in full bloom; it really looks like a lace doily that grandma use to make. It has a bright dainty white circular shape with many tiny white flowers intertwining together as if a loving grandma crocheted it. The beauty of nature was always all around on the farm.

Sweet Corn Time

The tassels were out in full glory and the tiny ears were growing their golden silk and every day I would check an ear of corn with much excitement of hoping to be the first farmer to have sweet corn ready.

This was my cash crop that Dad let me raise on my own for a little spending money. If my corn was ready before anyone else's, I would get first crop prices. I figured you might as well try to get as much as you could if you were doing it, so I always tried to be the first to have sweet corn for sale.

Setting up my sweet corn stand always put excitement in the air, and even the as the cars drove by I would see the smiles of the people as they drove past. People would stop before we had the corn picked! Making signs was an important part of getting the word out. Once we were ready, the picking began. Going into that first piece of sweet corn and stepping in between the rows, you knew it was ready by that special distinctive sweet smell that only existed in a ready sweet corn field. Grabbing that first ear of corn and pulling it down with a snap, the harvest began. One dozen, two dozen. Fill them crates, the race was on. Putting that first corn on the stand was an experience in itself. Your hopes and dreams of getting rich were about to come true! We all know you really can't get rich but the thought of every ear you picked getting turned into cash would let your imagination run just a bit. I guess the fact I was just a kid when I started selling sweet corn is what gave me that childish thought. To this day though, the thrill of opening the sweet corn stand for the season is a tradition that personifies the culmination of experiencing a sense of satisfaction that can be only found when you directly give from your hand to your customer's hand that dozen ears of corn that you nurtured with the help of mother nature and the one up above.

Selling corn is a great way to learn the basics of marketing. Good quality corn almost sells itself, but not quite. You need to attract your customer in order for them to stop and try it. So I used my artistic ability and made giant sweet corn ears out of plywood painted them bright green and yellow. They did the trick, because people would see them far enough in advance while driving they would have time to slow down and stop. Once they tasted our corn word would get around and all we had to do was keep picking! Rain or shine every day until the corn was done, early morning picking was now a routine.

Whenever I brought up some new corn from the field in the afternoon and restocked the stand, there always seemed to be a flurry of customers. The thought of the corn being fresh picked surely had something to do with it. I always enjoy visiting with the customers, the old timers wanted to know what variety the corn is, the Lakers want to know if they would get a discount on a large quantity. Then there is the customer that wants to buy two ears and still get an extra one free. Learning about the many different kinds of people is an adventure, especially for a farm boy!

I would especially enjoy when a teacher from school would stop and buy corn.

One of my favorites is Mr. Huff, also known as Father Huff to his former FFA students. Being a retired agricultural teacher at Livonia, he would show interest in farming when we conversed over the sale of a dozen ears. He would share his knowledge about farming and I was all ears, not that I did not have a few ears of corn in my hand!

As the corn season rolled on the corn got less abundant in the field. Between the raccoon damage and the smut, which is a type of fungus that grows on the tip of the ear, you had to look more carefully because the kernels were also getting tougher. Soon the Silver

Queen variety would be ready and picking will be easy with the plentiful large ears of milky white pure sugar kernels wrapped in a dark attractive green protective husk.

Yes, nothing like closing out the Labor Day holiday weekend with the cream of the crop, and a new large supply of it at that! Customers were pleased that we had Silver Queen and lined up to get their baker's dozen. The excitement of the holiday picnics definitely seemed to add to the many smiles and a friendly word or two with each dozen sold. I was smiling also because as much as I liked raising and selling corn, it was nice to be done for the season. After Labor Day school starts and corn on the cob and picnics come to an abrupt end, and summer is officially over. There is no doubt sweet corn is a very pleasurable part of many families summer vacation, and to think it all started last spring with the planting of the seeds in a field on my farm.

Back to School

Shopping for school clothes and supplies had to be done in order to be ready. Years ago here in downtown Livonia the local merchants were geared up for it. J.C. Monte carried boys and men clothing, and shoes, along with blue and orange school coats. Ray Fischer's Women and Men clothing carried quality dress clothes such as sweaters, suits, slacks etc. Paul's five and dime carried just about everything from school gym shorts to pens, paper and pencils. Paul's also carried shoes, sneakers and Buster Brown clothing, which were very popular with younger school children. If need be, these local merchants would put the bill on a slip for Ma or Dad to sign, no credit card needed. Just good old fashion trust along with a smile and friendly conversation.

These merchants were dependent of the farm families that made up most of Livonia at that time; they knew that when crops were harvested they would be paid. These are the ingredients that seem to all go together in the recipe of what it takes to make a community.

It must have worked because we had three grocery stores. They were Long's IGA, Harts Star Market, and Verne Graf's grocery and meat market. We also had Frank A. Rivers Furniture, The Milky Way Diner and ice cream bar, Rigney's Hardware Store, Struble Pharmacy, Firestone Store, Phil Sweeney Insurance, Meyer Chevrolet, Harry Ward Chrysler Plymouth Dealer, Rowland and

West Cars and service station, Tom Brennan's Barber Shop, Smitty's Barber Shop, Security Trust Bank, Livonia Hotel, Vallone Plumbing, Maurice Sweeney Real Estate, Trescott Jewelers, Livonia Lumber. Then there was Gibbs gas. Dad had gone to school with Bert Gibbs and of course our appliances were always bought from Gibbs. I am sure I missed a few other stores.

In essence what I am trying to say is that the small family farms were able to support the community well enough to have a numerous variety of business establishments. This in turn converted farm production into community commerce and a tax base for our town government, which in turn provided services to the people in general. Along with this our Livonia Central School was able to grow and meet the educational needs of the town's families.

Well all of the above information does not change the fact that us kids had to go back to school. The changing of our routine for chores and homework was not easy to get used to after all the freedom of summer vacation, but after a while things settled down just as they always seem to do after the first few days of school. I would find myself looking out the window on a sunny day though thinking about being outside and being able to get ready for silo filling time.

Silo Filling Time

No sooner you would be settled into school routine and the excitement of silo filling time arrived. After all, the silo corn was mature it had to be chopped and blown in the silo before a freeze. Chopped corn ensilage made good feed for dairy cows. Years ago Charlie Farrell would go around with his equipment and fill many a farmer's silo, including ours. However, now we had our own chopper and self-unloading wagon and my John Deere, the "Big Green Farming Machine." You needed a tractor with horsepower to be able to run our Papec corn chopper and pull the heavy self-unloading wagon at the same time. Now with our 3020 John Deere we had the power to get the job done.

Before we started chopping we had to ready the silo by putting the blower pipe up and secure it in place with a large rope tightened around the hoops of the silo. Hooking the pipe to the Allis Chalmer Blower was next; once this was done we put our Farmall H tractor in position to run the long pulley belt that turned the fan type propeller in the blower. Once lined up properly, belt dressing would be sprayed on the belt and we would run it for a while to make sure it run true.

The hollow wind sound blew up the silo pipe as the belt turned. This is the sound you would here through out the area during silo filling time, except the sound took on a loud fire cracker popping sound as chopped corn was unloaded into the blower and it was blown up and into the silo. The chopped corncob would hit the metal of the blower pipes at such speed the loud noise was almost deafening. The sound seemed to glorify the fact that corn was not only harvested but also in safe storage up in the silo now for feed this coming winter. The smell in the air was of sweet corn juice, and it only got sweeter as it would ferment in the silo. Sometimes there was so much juice in the corn, it would leak out of the silo staves and onto the ground around the silo. If any of this drained in the direction of where the cows were they would drink it up like corn whiskey!

It took about a week of chopping corn to fill a silo. Load after load Dad would disconnect the loaded wagon and connect the empty one. I would be on my way row after row. While I chopped, Dad would go up to the silo and unload; by the time he got back with the empty wagon I had the other one full. The roar of the tractor along with the sound of the corn being chopped echoed throughout our valley farm. Corn stubble in the field was all that was left after I went down the rows. The stalks and cob right to the tassel were now in the wagon all chopped nice and fine.

Once in a while the corn was so tall it would plug up before it went in the cutting box of the machine. This was a chore when it happened because it meant shutting down and hand pulling the stalks out. Once the machine was cleaned out the start up of the tractor resumed and once again the chopping of the corn could be heard echoing through out the valley. It was a welcome sound.

After school and weekends were now occupied by this effort to get the corn in the silo. The love of farming was the fuel that kept us steadfast in successfully getting our work accomplished. The work was actually part of our life so much that it became fun and provided a deep sense of satisfaction of father and son working together as a team.

I remember every year at this time Dad would recite a poem he had written:

> "The goldenrod is yellow,
> The fruit is bending down.
> Growing days are over,
> Harvest is abound."

Dad always seemed to recite it when I would be riding with him on the back of the tractor and we were going down the lane, where the goldenrod were in bloom and the wild apple trees were bending with their fruit. As I listened and looked at the same time, I felt how special this time of year was to all of nature, not just to us.

Regular chores of course had to be kept up, and cows having their calves did not wait. Well, a cow by the name of Old Muscato, decided to have her calf when our regular vet was out of town. A substitute vet was supposed to be on call. We could not reach him and by midnight this cow needed a vets help to deliver. Dad went up to the house and looked up Dr. Joseph O'Dea from Geneseo, even though he was a horse veterinarian, Dad thought perhaps he would help. Immediately Dr. O'Dea was up and in our barn in the middle of the night. He used his expert skills and successfully delivered a heifer calf and saved the cow. Dad was sending me up to the house for the checkbook when Dr. O'Dea said no need. He was a horse vet and he came just to help. He then shook our hands and was on his way. To this day I still can feel the warm appreciation we had that night for this good deed.

Winter Wheat

After the silo is filled it is time to put the plows back on and get the plowing done for the wheat ground. With the early fall weather being cool it seems to duplicate springtime conditions, but the days are getting shorter instead of longer. This is good weather to get the field ready for planting the wheat, which will winter over and continue growing in the spring.

There were Sea Gulls everywhere. They were all around my tractor, landing in groups on the fresh plowed soil, hunting once again as they did in the springtime. Their appearance seems to renew where I left off last spring, only this wheat won't be harvested until next July. From one growing season to the next, renewal and continuity mysteriously flows on just as nature intended it to.

With the field fitted nice and level and the rocks picked up, the fresh brown fitted soil looked as pretty as a picture and as level as a golf course. It was a sunny Christopher Columbus Day, and I was home from school. There I was, hooked up to our Ontario Grain drill. Dad was setting the rates for seed and fertilizer. There was a cold nip in the air, and you could see your breath. Dad and I both had our Carhardt's heavy jackets on; you had to be dressed for the weather this Columbus Day. There was not a cloud in the sky, and a good planting day seemed to be promised.

The covering chains made a jingle, as they were dragging on the ground behind the drill ever so lightly, doing their job of making sure the seed was well covered after being dropped into the soil by the drill's many discs. Once again round and round I went, stopping for refills of seed and fertilizer when needed. The heat off the tractor felt good today. Dad would ride on the platform board on the back of the drill now and then and make sure the seed was flowing properly.

This was our cash crop so we wanted it to be planted properly for maximum production. I remember sometimes this time of year being low on cash and having to make a visit to our hometown bank, where the manager Chet Haak would gladly lend us the money for the wheat seed and fertilizer and hold the note till harvest with just our signature and a hand shake, no paper work or applications. Sometimes this kind of help from your local banker is what kept you going from year to year.

Round and round the field until all of the land was planted. Then Dad would hook up the roller to pack it down and say "Lord willing, we will have a bumper crop next July." We would both smile knowing we did the job the best we could now it was up to the one up above and Mother Nature.

Fall Corn Harvest

The killing frost had come and gone and the corn had turned paper brown in color. The grain was now hard and golden yellow and the husk, which once fit snuggly around them, was loose and the ears were bending down just waiting to be picked.

We busily cleaned and repaired our corncribs. A corncrib consists of wood posts long and narrow with wire mesh stapled to boards making up a sturdy frame to hold the corncobs in. It is narrow because it is important that the wind can blow through providing a way for the corncobs to be dried completely and stay dry after they are harvested.

We used to have a neighbor farmer named Joe Morsch pick ours when it was time. When Joe was too busy Ronnie Smith and Leo Morsch would come. After we purchased our John Deere 3020 though, we purchased a New Idea 323 corn picker and two Kilbros grain wagons.

That moment of actually going out in the field with our own equipment to pick our corn was to me is forever etched in my memory. The day started out with a heavy frost leaving the aroma of cooking corn stalk leaves and husk as the sun warmed them. As I entered the cornfield that distinctive pleasant harvest time perfume filled the crisp autumn air. Dad was right behind me on his IH 424 pulling the grain wagon that would soon be hitched behind the picker that my Big Green Farming Machine would pull down row after row of corn. The gathering chains on the head of the picker would pull in the stalks of corn as two large rollers snapped the ears of corn off and into the husking bed. Quickly, the now bright yellow ears seemed to jump into the rotating paddles of the conveyer that would take them up in bunches of three or more to each paddle and dump them into the wagon.

The sight of watching this miracle of mechanization in the works as the bright yellow corn heaped higher and higher in the wagon created a spectacular sense of thrill for both Dad and I. Round and round the field I went, admiring the beauty of the autumn colors enveloping the surrounding fields. Here we were, part of nature's harvest with the bright yellow corn heaped high in the wagons. Even the colorful ring neck pheasants would grace us with their presence, as they would eat a stray kernel of corn that escaped the machine here and there. Spot would run along side exploring every nook and cranny in the harvested field. What was now left behind would feed nature's own from squirrels to deer, yes, even as we harvested our corn we seem to give back to nature a small token of appreciation for what Mother Nature had provided for us during the past growing season.

As each load was unloaded the corncribs became filled with the bright yellow ears of corn. The harvest time depended on the weather. Good dry weather was preferred. We always made time to pick our pumpkins for Halloween and to vote for Election Day. But a steady routine of picking the corn went on to about Thanksgiving. I can remember when it was that late in the season sometimes I would have to use the lights on the tractor after a days picking. Getting dark early meant winter was surely on it's way. We had a lot to be thankful for on Thanksgiving Day.

Flock after flock of geese would fly south as we put our machinery away for the season. Wintertime chores now made up the routine. It was once again snowy and cold on the farm and the warmth of the barn seemed good once again!

Christmas time was on its way for us to celebrate as a family this special time of year. Even the cows heard Christmas songs over the radio in the barn. We looked forward to New Year's Eve, and at midnight it was family tradition to go outside at see which way the wind was blowing, north, south, east or west. Dad always would predict if it was going to be a wet or dry, long or short growing season. Family, tradition and our community were basic ingredients to our farm recipe. As the year came to a close, a new one was just beginning, and so the cycle of the family farm continued.